MW01026993

CHOIR PRAYERS

To Eugene Englert,
whose choir was the inspiration
for these prayers.

Choir ※ Prayers

Jeanne Hunt

The Pastoral Press • *Washington, D.C.*

ISBN: 0-912405-22-8

The Pastoral Press
225 Sheridan Street, N.W.
Washington, D.C. 20011
(202) 723-5800

The Pastoral Press is the publications division of the National Association of Pastoral Musicians, a membership organization of musicians and clergy dedicated to fostering the art of musical liturgy.

Printed in the United States of America.

CONTENTS

INTRODUCTION

Choir Prayers was written to help parish choirs begin each rehearsal with a reflective moment. And, certainly, that is what personal prayer is all about—a time of reflection on the meaning of what we are doing.

Choir Prayers is not the prayer of public worship. The themes of the prayers of public worship are praise and thanksgiving, adoration and proclamation, penitence and confession. The themes of *Choir Prayers* are more modest and specific.

Choir Prayers is not the only way that a choir can pray. In fact, after reading through these prayers, you might find your own way to focus the attention of your parish choir on its particular needs and issues, on its elements of consciousness. Feel free to do so. In fact we encourage you to do so. We celebrate it when this model leads your choir to its prayer.

Our hope for *Choir Prayers* is that it will become a source book, leading you to encourage your choir to let the singing of the prayers of the church become its first and most important prayer. Our hope for *Choir Prayers* is that it will stimulate you and the other members of your choir to develop a regular moment during rehearsal when the attention of the choir is focused on what the choir is primarily doing, namely, praising and worshiping God through and in song.

Choir Prayers was developed by Jeanne Hunt in a real choir situation. When we began to organize these prayers for publication, we noticed (as you will) that there were very few prayers for Lent and none for Easter. Our first reaction was to solicit additional material for that most important season. And then we recalled the frantic reality of those rehearsals in our own experiences. It is the choir's busiest time. Is it also the time when you are most likely to need to pray? Or is it even the time when you might be most inclined to create your prayer for your own specific needs?

The National Association of Pastoral Musicians, a membership organization of musicians and clergy dedicated to fostering the art of musical liturgy, puts this book in your hands knowing that you will not use it slavishly, but will find in it a clue to deepening the prayer of your parish choir.

Rev. Virgil C. Funk
President
National Association of
Pastoral Musicians

Beginning the Choir Year

Welcoming In

*L*ord, we feel your welcoming in.
As the master of this house,
You open wide these doors to show us in.
You greet us with great warmth and affection,
    proud that we have come with our gift of song.
Like a gracious host you put us at ease.
For those of us who are returning this welcoming
    is a homecoming.
A coming back to the music we love,
    the challenge of what is to be.
For those of us who come for the first time
    tonight is the beginning of new song
    in our lives.
The kind of song that will drift through
    our minds and souls with the gentle prodding
    of God's Spirit.
Song that gives new grace and dimension
    to our days.
To each and everyone here, the Lord bids
    you his welcome with love.
May we serve you well, Lord.
Bless these gatherings of song.
Bless the generous hearts who come!
Amen.

All Things are Made New!

Lord, thank you for new beginnings.
You give us so many clean slates in our lives.
Times to return with a renewed energy,
  as if nothing had gone before.
You forget our failures as if they never existed.
Your vision is always for the present moment.
You do not look back.
You ask that we do the same.
This is the nature of your love.
We begin this musical year with that intention,
  Lord.
We envision the new music, the new harmonies,
  with a fresh enthusiasm.
This is our heritage as your children,
  a heritage of hope that allows us to look forward
  and not backwards.
Father, teach us this lesson of hope.
Teach us that you accept us right where we are,
  imperfect but getting better.
Last year's disasters are like a forgotten storm.
The Lord awaits our triumphs,
  the musical sunrises,
And so do we!

Miracles in Our Midst!

*L*ord, our numbers have dwindled!
There are just too many empty seats,
We want more voices to give fullness to the sound.
Yet strangely, Lord, as I listened to our
    music last Sunday,
    the sound was beautiful!
The balance was good.
I know our offering pleased and delighted you.
Could it be that our numbers suit you just fine?
Could it be that our sense of order
    and proportion are not yours?
You seem willing to take whatever we have and
    transform it into bounty.
No different than the small boy with
    loaves and fishes.
You seem to take our simple offering of sound
    and multiply and bless it.
Sometimes, we forget that you are a miracle
    worker.
And your miracles are still occurring in our
    everyday life.
You are working musical miracles in this choir.

If we have the eyes to see and the ears to hear.
It is so edifying to watch our loving God
    at work in this place.
A God who transforms our music.
Who still believes in miracles.
Who cannot resist a moment of grace.

Water Walking

"So Peter got out of the boat and walked on the water and came to Jesus, but when he saw the wind he was afraid and began to sink."   MT. 14, 29-31

Lord, give us courage to sing with assurance.
May we sing as if we know our music well,
     as if we are singing our part alone.
When we sing with uncertainty the sound
     betrays us.
Give us faith in ourselves and our gift.
Teach us to believe that we are capable of carrying
     our voice part even when the dependable leaders
     are absent.
It wasn't till Peter lost courage that his water
     walking failed.
As long as his eyes were on Christ and
     not on his own ability,
He was on the water and not in it!
Keep us above water, Lord.
May we focus anew on our Lord,
Remembering that what we do here is for him
     and not ourselves.

Our song is a prayer form, not a performance.
And there lies the difference.
Performers sing for self acclaim.
We sing for God.

So, Lord, give us the courage to do our own kind
    of water walking.
Just like Peter, we step out of the boat,
        a boat of security in singing quietly
        and following the strong voices.
Give us the faith to get that second foot
        out of the boat;
The first went out with ease!
Music is a form of water walking.
Bless our wet feet!

Amen.

Prayer Before a Choir Practice

*L*ord, bless those who give us the
harmony tonight.
Let us remember that theirs is the humble task
of lending a quiet texture to our melodies.
There is no shining glory in their role.
No one ever says how great those gentle
shading sounds are.
Yet, Lord, without that supporting depth the
glimmering heights of the melody fall lifeless.
Teach us to accept our own moments of
harmonizing.
Those times when you call us to be the servant
of the servants.
Each time we are asked to do a thankless,
unnoticed job,
let us have the wisdom to know that
you have seen our work and will thank
and bless us in your own way and time.
As we sing tonight, Lord, may we hear
each other anew.
May we hear and appreciate our harmony as the
gift it is—a quiet subtle offering to you
the One who blesses the humble of heart.

Amen.

The Wrong Notes

*L*ord, sometimes we sing the wrong note
and it seems so right!
No matter what our mind tells our voice to do,
it goes to that wrong note like bees to honey.
It just seems like the natural thing to do.
It's like original sin. We didn't mean to do it
but we're stuck with it.
The music stops. We are corrected.
We all agree that any knowledgeable person would
sing the right note.
We all conclude that it sounds so much better.
Then, we begin again and out of our mouths
comes the wrong note!
Lord, thank you for letting us see our humanness,
our vulnerability.
For if we could sing that right note with ease
we wouldn't need you so much.
Our lives are full of little wrong note kinds of sins—
a word of gossip, a little too much to eat,
an angry word.
Give us the grace to overcome the wrong notes
and the wisdom to remember who the Giver is.
Teach us to be patient with ourselves.
We are not perfect, yet.

We still need to be saved from the wrong notes!

"Sing to the Lord a New Song"

*L*ord, we love the miraculous moment when a
difficult work is finally sung with perfection.
Weeks of struggle and hard work, nights of
disenchantment and discouragement melt into
that fine moment of breathtaking beauty.
At first, we doubted it was possible.
The timing was beyond us.
The note spans were too taxing.
Yet we persevered, calling upon unknown resources.
Then, after such a difficult labor, we birth our song
in all its many-splendored wonder.
A new song thunders out among us!
We are at once awed and amazed at our work.

Lord, all the time you knew we could do it.
You upheld and supported our giftedness.
You watched our struggle with a father's love,
patiently believing in us when we did not
believe.

Lord, you prove to us, in this small way,
   what is possible in every part of our lives.
Your expectations are great for those you love.
You can turn our mustard-seed faith into
   mountain-top beauty.
You can take our small offerings and create a
   marvelous new song.

"Many Sheep I Have..."

*L*ord, we understand why you call your
  people sheep.
Sheep are some of the dumbest creatures you made!
It was your subtle way of implying that we aren't
     as smart as we think we are.
Yet, you are willing to shepherd our dumbest
     moments.
Music always gives us an opportunity to act
     like sheep.
When we least expect it we do something dumb —
     singing through a rest,
       being the only forte in a choir of pianos,
       singing the melody in bass clef while the other
       baritones sing harmony.
Lord, get us through our sheep-ish moments,
     tonight.
Thank you for teaching us the humbling lesson of
     accepting our mistakes.
Please shepherd this choir as we practice
     tonight, Lord.
Give us the wisdom to always keep in mind that we
     are sheep, and from time to time
     even the finest in the flock
     needs a little shepherding!

Spirit Song

*L*ord, we sing with a special purpose tonight.
Allow these melodies and hymns to be spirit
songs.

May we offer not only a pleasing sound, but a song
that will have the power to touch souls.

May we sing with the conviction that allows the
words to come from our hearts.

May Your Spirit breathe energy and power into
our words.

Let each song strike a new chord in the lives
of our listeners.

May these hymns provide inspiration as well as
pleasure.

And Lord, even as we ask this for our listeners
we ask this blessing for ourselves.

Never let the melodies and words become so
commonplace that they lose their fire
as we sing.

Let the hymns sound new in our ears.

May we pray as we sing.

Let the words become the prayers and thoughts
of our hearts.

Give a grace to our words that we might be
uplifted as we sing.

May the gift we give tonight be returned a
hundredfold.

Amen.

Advent and Christmas

"Prepare Ye the Way"

*T*onight, Lord, we begin our preparation
  for Christmas.
These are the wonder songs that proclaim the
  marvel of that moment of divine love.
We are privileged to enter this season once again.
A season in which our voices revel in the quiet awe
  of your humble birth.
Lullabys and gentle lyrics are our prayer as we
  sing to an infant no different in birth than
  the babies we have held.
Keep us in touch, Lord, with our task.
Our voices bring to this congregation the
  innocent wonder, the magnificent joy,
  the overwhelming love of this Jesus
  who became one among us.
Allow us to see him anew ~~in these Advent weeks;~~
See him as the child of love;
Sing to him with tender hearts.
For we can easily get lost in our busy ways...
So much music to learn, so little time, so many
  Christmas chores.
Help us spend these Advent rehearsals as a time
  apart in your presence,

Let us

Never forgetting the beauty and simplicity of that
   holy night.
A night that changed our lives.
A night that deserves the voices of angels!

"One Can Hear the Falling Snow..."

*I*t's hard to sing about snow when it's raining
and warm outside.
We want to feel the magic of the season,
but the world is not cooperating.
I used to pray for a white Christmas.
I loved the sparkle-wonder feeling of new-fallen
snow.
The white quiet created in me a mystical sense
of the holy night.
Snow is a spectacle from heaven,
a marvelous backdrop for the birth night.
However, snow on Christmas is rare in these parts.
We have learned to make our peace with the
grey-brown days that grace your birth.
Lord, you have taught me, in my disappointment,
that all those snow feelings have nothing
to do with the weather.
They are feelings of the heart.
A heart that has fallen in love with the season
and its precious King.
So, for us each Christmas is white in an
invisible way.
We choose to see beyond the grey-brown of earth
to a heavenly vision.

Lord, as we sing about snow in these Christmas
    hymns, help us to see beyond our surroundings
    to the places of the heart.
The heart where Christ lives.
All feelings of a snowy night abide there.
One can hear the falling snow in the
    places of the heart.

Come Lord Save Your People

*L*ord, our time grows short and the work ahead
seems beyond us.
We are hard pressed to learn so much music in the
hours left us.
We come to you tonight, asking for a special grace.
Allow your Spirit to fill us anew with the power
to learn quickly and well.
Let us sing with certain voices.
Give us the peace that comes from being
well prepared.
May this peace that surpasses all understanding be
ours as we allow you to give us the wisdom
and gift to sing well.
You must be the source of our strength.
We yield to your powerful, abiding presence.
We will allow your Spirit to sing through us
tonight,
Sing a perfect holy song . . . a Spirit song.
A song that comes easily because you are
the source.
Steady our anxious hearts and make a quick work
of our task.

May we give you our voices, hearts, and minds
in this rehearsal time, so that what is impossible
for us may occur with divine ease!
We ask that Christmas night be filled with glorious
praise-song,
not because we struggled but because we trusted
enough
to allow your Spirit to work a marvelous deed.

A Final Prayer Before Christmas

*L*ord, bless these final moments of
preparation.
We have spent our Advent preparing a foundation
of practice.
We have refined our music.
We have given it time and discipline.
Now, the final touches are necessary.

Keep us sensitive to the lyrics of our hymns.
Our music and its words have the power to turn
minds to Christ if they are sung
with conviction.
Our voices blended in love for you can win hearts
that have long ago forgotten the message
of this feast.

Teach us, tonight, to sing to a whisper when
the moment needs it.
Our quiet song can fill this church with a
peace that does not exist outside these doors.
When forte is asked for, let us not shout for
our own sakes, but sing in bold strength
that shatters the air with praise!

Give us your rhythm, Lord.
A spiritual rhythm that gives heartbeat to our
    music.
May our sense of timing subtly underline the song
So that the mood and meaning of our song
    will cause the listener to move with our sound.
Fill us with the rhythm of angels who filled the sky
    that first holy night.
The pace of heaven that transcends the human
    heart.
Let us sing in unhurried peace to Jesus,
    the cause of our praise.

Lord, accept our gift of song tonight.
For we offer it to you from our hearts.
It is the finest gift, more precious than any
    we have under our trees.
It is a part of us, given because we really
    and tenderly love you.

Through
the Winter

Blessed Are...
A Choir Prayer for the New Year

*C*hristians do not have a new year's resolution,
They have blessed are...
It works the same in concept,
yet without the guilt of broken resolutions.
Jesus started it all one afternoon on a mountain.
It had definite crowd appeal and
is still popular today.
As we begin this new year, Lord,
we offer you our own blessed are...
We ask for your grace and strength as we
struggle with them:

— Blessed are those who always show up,
for theirs is the peace and integrity of a
faithful servant.
— Blessed are those who remember to compliment
others for a well-done effort,
for they too shall succeed.
— Blessed are those who look at the director instead
of gluing their eyes to the notes,
for they shall sing with sensitivity.
— Blessed are those who mean the words they sing
and pray them, for they have the power
to move the heart of their listener.

– Blessed are those who clearly pronounce their
    words, for they shall be
    understood and appreciated.
– Blessed are those who stay in pitch, for they shall
    be called blessed by the director!
– Blessed are those who do not shout but rather
    sing in a spirit of full and powerful forte,
    for they shall be blessed with an
    understanding of praise.
– Blessed are those who sing in their range,
    for they shall be humble in the
    kingdom of heaven.

Winter Prayer

*I*n the quiet stillness of this winter night we praise
you, Lord.
You are the Lord of our music.
The author of all that creates our sound.
As we sing we return to you in a many-splendored
display the gifts you have so generously poured
out in this choir.
How blessed we are to have this straightforward
way of praising you.
How blessed we are to have the vehicle of music to
make our praise tangible.
So often words cannot express the images of our
hearts and the wordless beauty of song-praise
raises to the heavens our deepest feelings.
Music in itself is a most wondrous gift of praise.
Thank you for the ears to hear it and the voices to
lend to it.
Keep us always mindful, Lord, that we are here
not so much to enjoy this gift for ourselves.
We are here to give it away so that other ears
might know what we have known,
other spirits soar to the heights, as ours have,
other hearts be touched by your love,
as ours have.

Sing A New Song... A Hymn to (

*L*ord, there have been many songs in our lives.
As children our songs were the sing-song
   rhythms of fantasy and delight.
In our youth we were lost in the songs of our day,
   the songs that proclaimed our feelings,
   feelings that others couldn't understand.
Later, we sang the songs of our ideals... beauty,
   patriotism, justice, mercy...
We were caught up in the idealism of youth.
Then we sang our love songs,
   the beautiful melodies for the other,
   the one who made such songs have meaning for
   the first time.
Sweet lullabys and gentle words grace our lives as
   we cradle the newborn.

Now, dear Lord, we come to this church to sing
   a new song.
Not a song rising out of our own need,
   our own life rhythm.
Rather a hymn to our God, a song of a higher
   stature, a greater depth.
We are called beyond ourselves to sing a
   hymn of praise.

No matter what the different songs of our lives,
  we share in common the call to praise,
We come together to sing this new song because we
  know you as a loving and faithful God.
We wish to give you our greatest song...
  "a new song... a hymn to our God."

Tested Like Gold

*L*ord, you seem to be testing us.
　　Our confidence wanes in the midst
　　of our struggle.
Things that we simply took for granted are
　　now coming hard.
Our ears strain to clue our voices to that subtle
　　change in pitch.
We are frustrated and at a loss for a solution to the
　　ills that plague us.
We yearn to sing unencumbered by this burden.
You test our gift, our spirit, our very commitment.

"My people, the finest jewel, the most precious
　　metal must endure the fire to become the
　　rare treasure.
So it is with the gift of song.
I call you to humble yourselves in refinement
　　of your voice.
Is not the fruit ripened only because of the pruning
　　and the long heat of the sun?
I mean to challenge everything about
　　your spirit-song.
So that the final fruit may be pure.
A song that is unblemished and refined.

A song meant for heaven.
This labor does not come easy.
You must strip yourself of pride and be willing
    to hear the flaws.
I will support and uplift you as you humble
    yourself in correction.
My hands are those of the potter.
If you love me you will yield as clay.
I allow these testing times out of my eternal
    love for you.
Remain faithful to your call.
I am even now pouring out a new sound
    in your midst.
Your pruning will yield much fruit."

There Are Many Gifts But One

*L*ord, the people in this choir are as varied in
their gifts as the flowers of the field.
And oh, how you love the differences!
There are the full voices who sing with confidence
and gusto
. . . and God loves their brazen beauty.
There are the soft voices who sing like the winds
of spring in their gentle, lyric ways
. . . . and God loves their fragile sweetness.
There are the harmonizers, who hear those rich
dark notes as a second nature
. . . and God loves their sensitive, humble ways.
There are those whose pitch never wavers
. . . and God loves their integrity and clarity.
There are those who struggle with pitch
. . . and God loves their courage and commitment.
There are those older voices who sing with the
polished beauty of wisdom
. . . and God loves them for their faithfulness.
There are the young voices who sing with
confidence and abandon
. . . and God loves them for their enthusiasm
and excitement.

Yet, Lord, let us remember that for all our varied
 ways each of us belongs here.
We make up the splendid weave of a choral sound,
 and not one among us is greater in your sight.
Even as we cherish our own giftedness,
Teach us to love what is beautiful in the other.
To love as you have loved . . . and no less!

Lent

The Tempo of Lent

*L*ord, the somber notes of Lent surround us.
We sing the songs of sorrow, grief, compassion,
and death.
How strange it is that such morose themes have
such enticing beauty.
Even as the tempo slows, the harmony darkens.
So too, do our spirits enter the shadow places
of these lenten days.
Lord, we find no less splendor in these songs
than the triumphant alleluias that are to come.
Give us renewed wisdom to understand the wonder
of the cross.
May our music betray our faith in the paschal
mystery . . . without death there is no life.
The glory of this music is that it proclaims our
heritage, our communion with the suffering
Christ.
We pray for the grace to see his suffering anew,
to sing our sorrow song with faith,
to allow our voices to betray our hearts,
hearts won by him in a piercing death cry!

"The Flesh Is Weak!"

*L*ord, the pageantry of Holy Week time is nothing
new to us.
How many times have we heard the passion
narrative?
For years we have listened to these ceremonies.
We have sung through these rituals from our
earliest days.
It is not with much enthusiasm that we face
another Easter week.
The services are long and demanding.
Left to our own weak wills we might stay away.
We can certainly relate to the sleepers in the garden
that Thursday night!

So, Lord, we come to you tonight with our
very human needs.
Lift us up beyond ourselves.
Allow these ageless words to burst into a
spirit-filled pathos for us.
Let it be not so much the tired motions,
the predictable story that we hear,
But some new word . . . The Word . . . in all its
power overcoming this tired ritual.
May we meet you at Calvary.

May our voices and hearts transcend the events
   in this church
And sing instead with a power that is inspired
   by your Spirit.
Lift our spirits toward a heavenly reality.
May our weary bodies and old melodies find energy
   and meaning as we see the face of our
   suffering Jesus.
The spirit is willing... the flesh is weak.
Tonight, Lord, we give you both.
Our flesh, our voices to be used again in this
   ancient liturgy.
Our spirits waiting like parched earth to be
   touched by your Spirit.

"Made In The Image And Likeness"

*L*ord, how diverse and splendid are the melodies
  we sing.
Each song is unique to itself,
  like nothing heard before.
What a wonder it is that men and women continue
  to create new, unheard music.
Like snowflakes and thumbprints that are never
  alike,
Creation continues in human works.
The Father-Creator joins with the Spirit to sing a
  new unending song through the channels
  of humankind.
Each composer brings forth something unsaid,
Something ears have never heard for all time,
And God is magnified in their efforts.
How beautifully, wonderfully made are we!
So privileged to be made in the image and likeness
  of God.
A creator who delights in our song.
Who anticipates with us each new work.
We praise you Creator-Spirit for such unending
  beauty, stemming forth from the seed gift
  you have planted in us.

Ending
the Year

"The Winter is Over,
The Flowers Appear in our Land"

*W*inter is beyond us now, Lord, and our spirits
  rise with the coming of spring.
Your flamboyant outburst of life affects us
    as we come here to sing.
The sweet heaviness of the air changes our mood
The excitement of our Easter Alleluias fades
    as we hear a softer piano on the earth.
We see the gentler side of our God as music turns
    from vibrant white to pastel.
This is a time aside where we are compelled to stop
    our busy ways and revel in the wonder around
    us.
For those of us who yield to the wonder a moment
    of grace will occur.
Lord, keep us simple enough to enjoy this spectacle.
Teach us that the greatest wisdom is found in a
    simple response to life.
Our music is betrayed by the spirit in which we
    sing.
Those who are insensitive to the wonder of life
    have no vibrance in their song...
    only the mechanics of sound.

Yet, those who fill their souls with the inspirations
of life give their music a fourth dimension that
is heard in the heart of the listener.
Lord, give this choir that dimension.
Grant that our song will foretell the wonder of life
around us.
May this spring not go unnoticed by us singers.
Let us take it in as food for our song!

4-18

Prayer For Perseverance

L ord, it has been a good year.
We have relished the challenge.
Delighted in the beauty of our music.
We have struggled and been pushed beyond
  our limits.
All this was exciting and well worth the effort,
  but now we are tired.
The feasts are over and the warmth of the
  oncoming summer lulls us into a yearning
  for rest.
We want to take it easy
  and you are asking for more.
How often in our lives you have asked us to give
  beyond our limits.
You ask not so much for what comes easy
But for the time, energy, and effort that come hard.
Our love and dedication are tested,
  not by the giving of the gift of small price
  but rather by the unselfish laying down
  of our treasures.
Now is the testing time.
Now, our discipleship, our call to this choir is tried.
~~Our numbers have already decreased.~~
How attractive our diversions seem.

Yet, our task here is not finished.
The final notes have not been sung.
So tonight, Lord, our prayer is for perseverance.
Grace us with the strength to continue to serve
   you.
Serve you now, when the giving comes hard.

Amen!

"Holy God We Praise Thy Name..."

*L*ord, last Sunday I watched our congregation
   at song.
What a sight I beheld!
It was as if, for a brief moment, I saw with your
   eyes the people you love.
There were old singers, mother singers, blue-collar
   singers, little girl singers, heartfelt singers, and
   lip service singers.
A myriad of life's blending in worship song.
Some cared about what they said and sang
   with purpose.
Some couldn't have cared less and sang in
   half-hearted style.
Yet, you, Father God, delighted in them all,
Because you know and love them far beyond
   my understanding.
Then I noticed a young man standing next to
   his older brother.
Neither was singing.
Suddenly, the older realized his brother was silent.
And, as if to lead by example, joined the chorus.
"Infinite Thy vast domain..."

Both brothers sang together, with lips barely parted.
How dear was that feeble effort in your sight.
More gracious a gift than the robust voices
     of we the choir.
Not because their hymn was as lovely as ours,
     but because it took courage and choice
     and ours did not.
They ran out the door as the last chord sounded,
     anxious to get back to their adolescent world.
Yet, I felt you rejoice over their gift,
     as if a rare and priceless treasure had been left
     in the church that morning.
A treasure you mean a hundredfold someday
     to return.
Someday when they need your song in their lives.
And you will gladly sing to them because
     you will remember this day.

Reed of God

*L*ord, it is Pentecost.
We meet, again, that Spirit
who alone blows the fire into our minds,
our hearts,
our voices.
That celebrated energy of the church,
Whose very name expresses what has drawn
generations into these walls to meet their God.
It is vibrant Life.
It is Fire.
It is Breath.

Our song is not of us,
rather it is the song of your Spirit.
We are like hollow reeds, which you have pierced
with holes.
In the piercing, in life's pain, we give to you
our very substance.
That is the way of Love.
You hone and craft us well, so that, finally, we
become an instrument in your hands.
You take the reed,
Blow your magnificent breath through it,
and Spirit song is created.

Father, confirm us anew in our gift of song.
We are singers,
   reeds in your hand.
Let us never forget that without your breath
   the reed is lifeless,
   and there is no song.
May we inspire those who hear us to come to you.
Not because we sang,
but because they heard God's Spirit.

Amen.

The Final Rehearsal

*L*ord, this is our final rehearsal of the year.
We celebrate it and regret it.
This has been a demanding year.
There has been painful growth,
   and a new respect for one another.
There was marvelous sound
   and untold creative accomplishments among us.
We have grown as singers, as friends,
   as saints because of our year together.

Now it is finished and we have a hiatus.
A quiet time of rest.
No less than when Christ went into the desert,
   do we go into rest.
Even singers must "be still and know that I am
   God."
May this desert time come as blessed refreshment.
Allow us to come back to this choir
   with a new excitement and energy.
Our cups have been emptied in service to you.
We leave now to refill them.
Fill them with the fire of your Spirit,
   the grace of knowing you,
   the sweet wine of your Love,
   and the peace that is our privileged gift.

Amen.